Make things Grandma made

Marjorie Stapleton

Taplinger Publishing Co., Inc.
New York

Acknowledgments
Photographs on pages 16, 44, 56 and 59 are crown copyright and
appear by permission of the Victoria and Albert Museum.

First published in the United States in 1975 by
TAPLINGER PUBLISHING CO., INC.
New York, New York

Library of Congress Catalog Card Number: 74-21672
ISBN 0-8008-5052-1

Contents

Note to American Readers

The following terms may be unfamiliar to some American readers and are accordingly clarified below to facilitate the use of this book:

chemist – pharmacist
cochineal – use red food coloring
cocktail stick – tooth pick
Copydex – adhesive similar to Elmer's Glue-All
Demerara sugar – similar to coarse brown sugar
dolly pegs – wooden clothes pins

Introduction

Grandma was always as fresh as a daisy, neat as a pin and even busier than a bee. You had to be a very early bird indeed to catch her lighting her candle to start the day.

Her little house, shining like a new penny, was a treasure box of home made bits and pieces. With fifteen children tied to her apron strings she had to be thrifty. Patchwork quilts and cushions and rag rugs all came out of the rag bag, not to mention Willie's best suit from the old parlour curtains. Scraps of all kinds, fancy papers, feathers, ribbons, trimmings and old boxes were never thrown away.

Although she swept, cooked, mended, sewed and baked from dawn till dusk, she never forgot treats like toffee apples, sugar mice, peg dolls and even edible stained glass windows.

It is a long time since then. My Grandma could have been your great or even great great Grandma but, as there is nothing really new under the sun, I thought you might like to try your hand at making some of the things that Grandma made.

M.S.

Stained glass windows

On rainy days, Grandma and her children made stained glass windows. They smelt delightful when freshly cooked and were very good to eat. Sometimes they were kept just to look through.

The best days to make them were baking days, when scraps of pastry left over from the large family's many pies could be transformed into architectural gems.

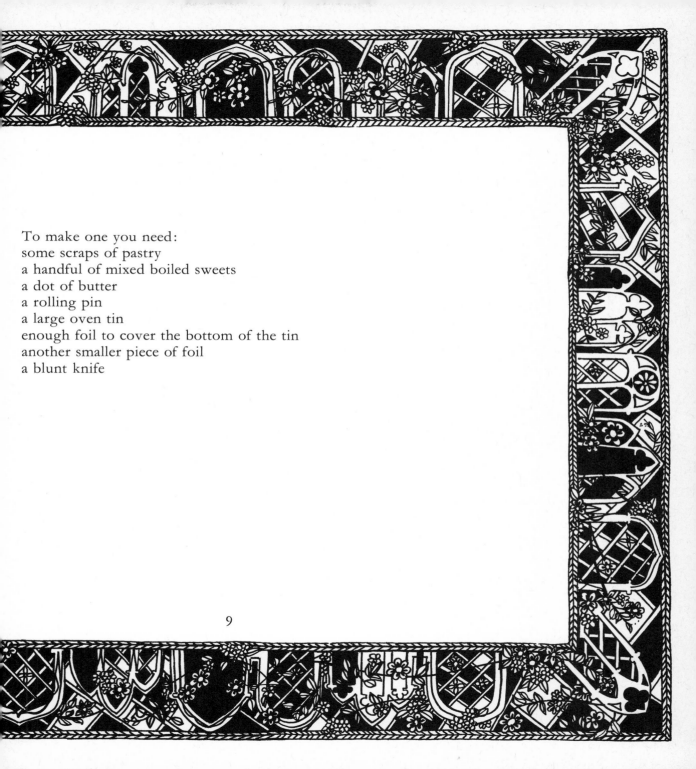

To make one you need:
some scraps of pastry
a handful of mixed boiled sweets
a dot of butter
a rolling pin
a large oven tin
enough foil to cover the bottom of the tin
another smaller piece of foil
a blunt knife

9

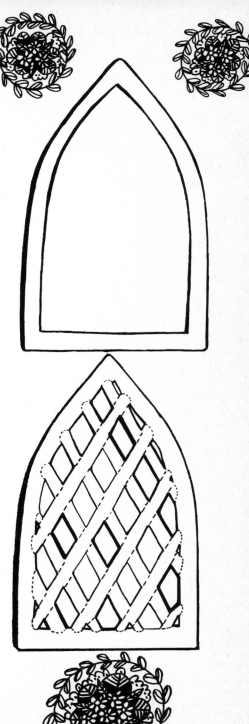

Roll out your pastry on a floured board or table.

Cut two long strips and one shorter one to make the frame.

Spread the large piece of foil over the bottom of the oven tin and rub the dot of butter on it.

Make a church window shape with the strips of pastry on the foil. Wet the joins with a drop of water and press them firmly together.

Cut up the rest of the pastry into thinner strips and make a criss-cross pattern with them in your window frame.

Dip your finger in water again and moisten the underside of the top layer of strips. Then press firmly wherever they cross, so that the molten window panes will stay separate in the cooking.

Now wash your hands and wipe away all traces of flour from the board or table, leaving a clean surface to work on.

If your sweets are wrapped, leave the wrapping on them and give each a smart tap with the rolling pin. If they are unwrapped, take your spare foil, tear it into small squares and wrap each sweet separately. Then hammer each in turn.

Carefully pour the broken pieces into the window spaces, making a pretty arrangement of colours. Fill each space as full as you can but try not to spill any pieces on the frames. Press them gently down with the flat side of your knife.

Put the tin in the oven. The middle of a warm oven is best, (400°F, gas mark 5). Do not have the oven any hotter or your colours will be dingy.

Cook for about fifteen minutes. You can look in from time to time to see how things are. Take the tin out as soon as the pastry is cooked. Cooking for too long also dims the colours.

Stand it in a cool place until it is completely cold, then peel off the foil and you have your stained glass window.

If you want to impress the vicar you might like to try other shapes.

12

Look in a book on architecture for more ideas. You will find church windows with interesting names such as Norman, Early English or Decorated.

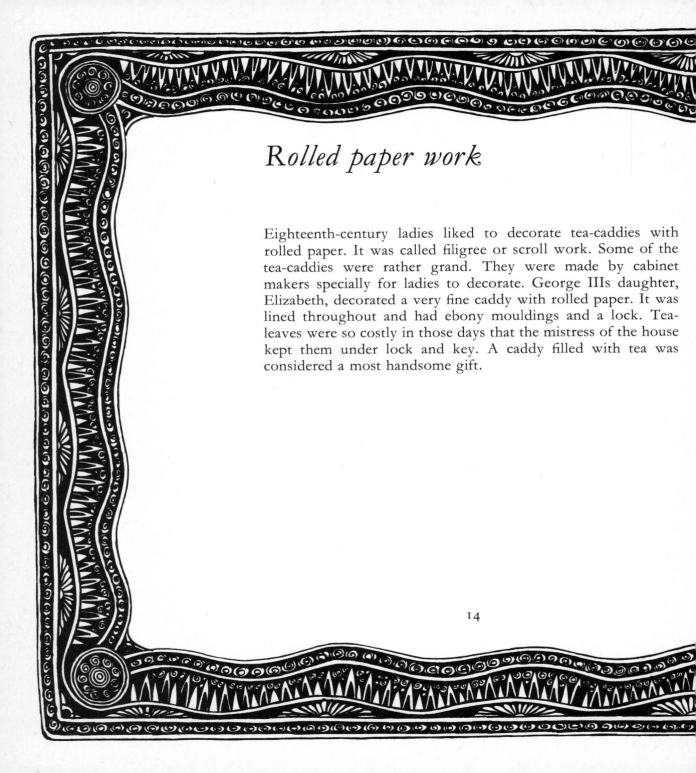

Rolled paper work

Eighteenth-century ladies liked to decorate tea-caddies with rolled paper. It was called filigree or scroll work. Some of the tea-caddies were rather grand. They were made by cabinet makers specially for ladies to decorate. George IIIs daughter, Elizabeth, decorated a very fine caddy with rolled paper. It was lined throughout and had ebony mouldings and a lock. Tea-leaves were so costly in those days that the mistress of the house kept them under lock and key. A caddy filled with tea was considered a most handsome gift.

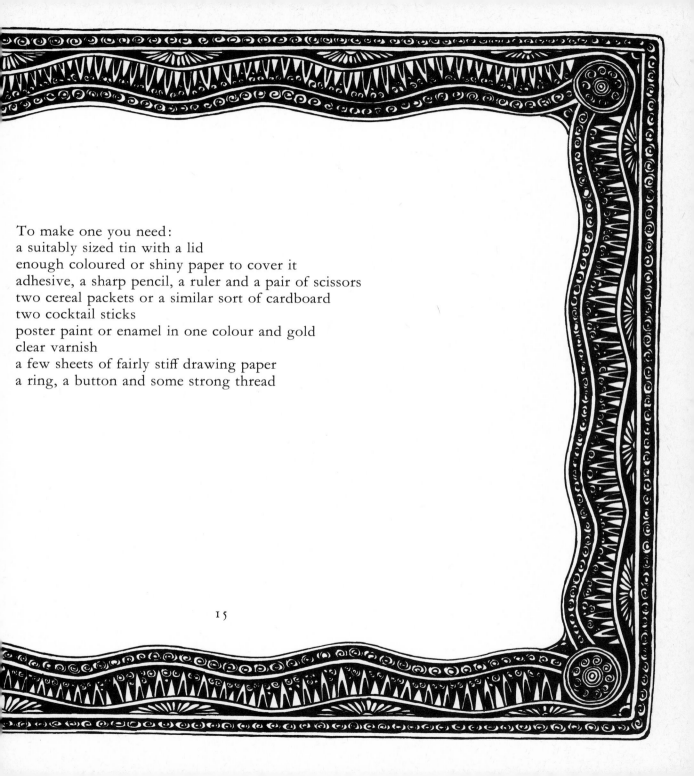

To make one you need:
a suitably sized tin with a lid
enough coloured or shiny paper to cover it
adhesive, a sharp pencil, a ruler and a pair of scissors
two cereal packets or a similar sort of cardboard
two cocktail sticks
poster paint or enamel in one colour and gold
clear varnish
a few sheets of fairly stiff drawing paper
a ring, a button and some strong thread

Stick your coloured or shiny paper round the tin and on top of the lid.

Cut the card into strips about 1·5 cm. (½ in.) wide and long enough to reach round the tin.

Put the lid on the tin. Paste a strip of card round the base and another immediately below the lid.

Stick five more strips on top of each of these so that you have two thick rims. Try to make the top layer of card the neatest.

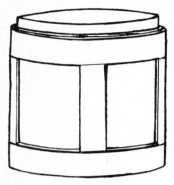

Glue more strips lengthways between the two thick rims. These will divide the tin into sections to hold your scroll patterns. Build up these new strips to make them as thick as the two rims.

Build a rim round the outside of the lid in the same way so that it fits neatly with the rim on the tin. But make this rim stand up a little higher than the top of the tin to form a hollow on top of the lid. This will contain more scroll work.

Clean off any dried paste and generally tidy up all your cardboard rims, paying particular attention to the joins. If you need to you can shave tiny bits off the rims or let small shavings into any gaps. Try to make it absolutely perfect.

Paint the strips of cardboard with coloured paint. If you are using poster colour, varnish it when it is dry.

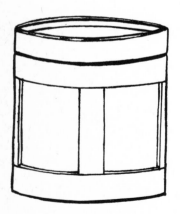

Cut the drawing paper into very narrow strips about 10 cm. (4 in.) long.

Wind one round the end of a cocktail stick. Add a small dot of paste with the other cocktail stick to stop it unwinding. Lift it off when completed. This is your scroll.

Make a few more. You will soon find that you get very quick at it – which is just as well, as you are going to need a few hundred.

When you have made about five or six, try them for size in a corner of one of your tin spaces. When in place they should stand up level with the cardboard rims but no higher.

Stand them on end side by side, as close together as you can. Glue them firmly down onto the coloured or shiny paper.

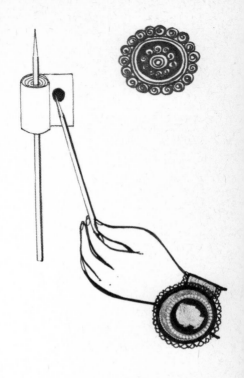

19

You can make your scroll patterns as simple or ornate as you wish. To divide up the areas of scrolls, you can use leaves, petals, rings, zig-zags, or anything else of your own invention. Make these from strips of drawing paper the same width as the scrolls. If you need to make the paper more pliable for gentle curves, try pulling the strips over the sharp edge of your scissor blade for a few moments before making up the shape.

Sometimes the maker would include her initials in the decoration, and sometimes spaces were left to hold little panels of embroidery, or perhaps initials and flower sprays. Miniature paintings were also used in this way.

When you have filled all the spaces on the tin, puncture a small hole in the centre of the lid.

Tie some strong thread onto the ring and thread it through the hole, leaving the ring on top.

Now thread it through the button underneath the lid and tie the ends together. The ring will stand up properly when you have packed your scroll pattern into the lid compartment.

Finish off the scroll work all over the top of the lid.

Some people liked to leave their scrolls plain and some liked to touch the edges lightly with gold paint. You can do as you wish, perhaps trying out some gold on a few experimental scrolls made separately, before you decide.

When the scroll work is perfectly dry and cleaned up to your complete satisfaction, give it a coat of thin clear varnish.

It will have been a lot of hard work, but you will have something very nice to keep, or give to your favourite person.

Pressed flowers and fruit peel flowers

Grandma was very romantic about flowers. Like many Victorian people, she knew what each flower was supposed to mean.
If you received a dahlia you knew the sender was for ever yours. Similarly, an anemone meant fading hope; a primrose 'I'm more faithful than you'; and a snapdragon reproved you for being dazzling but dangerous.

Flowers were pressed and preserved to make delicate pictures and love tokens.

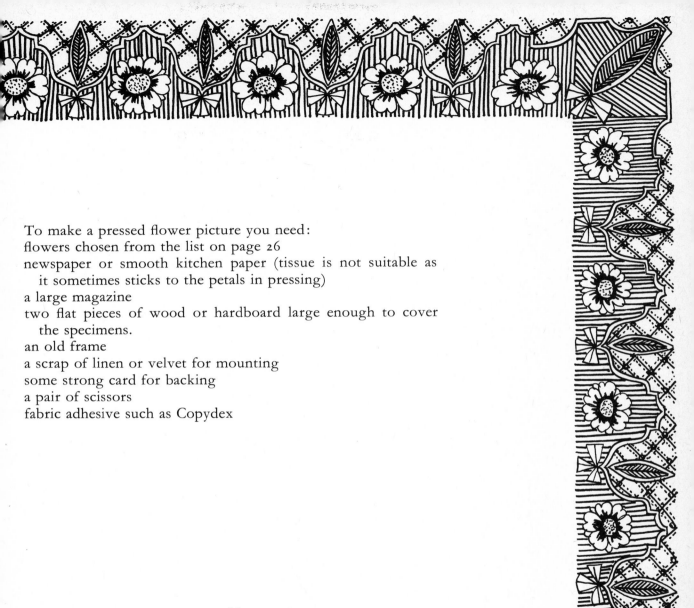

To make a pressed flower picture you need:
flowers chosen from the list on page 26
newspaper or smooth kitchen paper (tissue is not suitable as
    it sometimes sticks to the petals in pressing)
a large magazine
two flat pieces of wood or hardboard large enough to cover
    the specimens.
an old frame
a scrap of linen or velvet for mounting
some strong card for backing
a pair of scissors
fabric adhesive such as Copydex

Pick the flowers at midday on a hot sunny day when the surface moisture will have dried off them.

Cut a small folder from your absorbent paper for each flower. Make sure the paper is perfectly dry as any dampness will turn the petals brown.

Arrange the flowers in the folders, taking great care over position as this is how they will look when they are pressed. Try to plan at this stage the way you would like them in the final picture. Do not forget extra leaves.

Place the folders between the pages of the magazine. You can slip one in between every ten pages.

Put the magazine between the two pieces of wood and place it somewhere warm and dry with four heavy books on top.

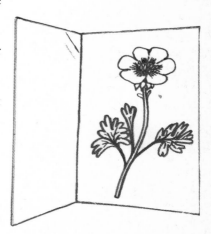

Small flowers take a few days, and larger varieties a week or two.

Some retain their colours much better than others. The most successful are listed over the page.

Pansy (press for three days)

Heather, lavender, delphinium, daisy, snowdrop, primrose, buttercup, hydrangea, poppy (press for five days)

Mimosa, geranium, cornflower, rose, clover, forget-me-not, sweet William, fern (press for seven days)

Anemone (press for ten days)

Chrysanthemum (press for fifteen days)

Skeleton leaves were often used for a pretty effect, either with pressed flowers or on their own. Making a skeleton leaf is quite easy. You need: firm leaves such as laurel or magnolia, a handful of washing soda, a blunt knife and an old pan.

Fill the pan with water and add the soda. Put in the leaves and bring them to the boil. Then let them simmer gently for an hour. This will soften the green tissue.

Take the leaves out and, very carefully, scrape the green away with your knife, leaving the veins.

Wash them gently in clear water. Then lay them on card and blot them with smooth absorbent paper. These, of course, do not need pressing.

If you have an old frame, cut a piece of board or strong card to fit it and stretch your background fabric over it. Secure the fabric at the back of the card with adhesive or large stitches.

26

Try to make it very taut and even at the front.

Now arrange your picture, sticking down the pressed flowers with minute dots of adhesive.

If you have no frame, a velvet ribbon can look pretty fixed round the edge on double-sided sticky tape. Fold the ribbon to make mitred corners (see diagram). Finish it with a small bow or rosette at the centre top or bottom. The flowers do not necessarily need to be covered with glass, though it does protect them from dust. Also it is a good plan not to hang your picture in direct sunlight as the delicate colours might fade.

Fruit peel flowers

Surprisingly strong but fragile looking flowers were made from orange and lemon skins. They looked rather like parchment and were used to decorate trays, bowls, bookends, shelves and all sorts of Victorian odds and ends. Also, mounted up in a box frame, they made attractive wall decorations.

To make them you need; Oranges and/or lemons, a blunt knife, sharp scissors, clear varnish, thin strong glue and any small seeds, peppercorns, dried peas or barley that you might have.

Cut the fruit in half and remove the pulp to eat.

Carefully scrape out the white pith with the knife and your fingernails until you get down to a pattern of fine lines close to the outer skin.

Now hold your shell under the cold tap for a few minutes to clean out all the bits.

With the sharp scissors cut the skin into any flower and leaf shapes that you like.

Put all your bits and pieces on an oven tray and into an oven at the lowest temperature you can possibly manage with the oven door closed.

They have to stay in the oven for four or five hours, so make sure before you start that it is not going to be needed for cooking.

28

Look in occasionally to see that it is not too hot, as too high a temperature will cause them to go brown and brittle. Leave the door open if you think this is starting to happen.

When they are thoroughly dried out you will find that they have twisted and curled into attractive natural looking shapes.

Now you can stick them together as you like, using the small seeds as centres.

If you would like to put them in a box frame, but haven't got the real thing, look round for an old wooden lid. The sort of box that chocolate liqueurs are sometimes packed in at Christmas would make a very attractive frame.

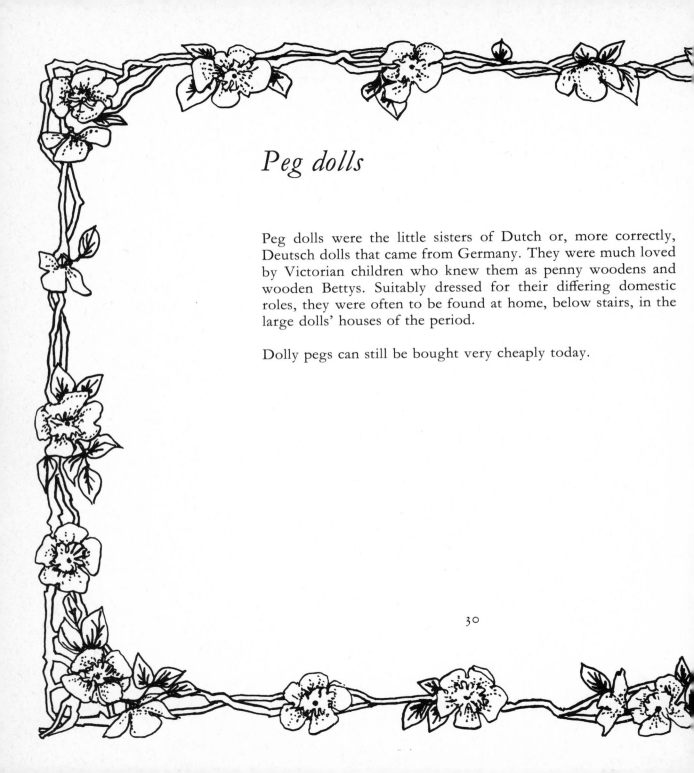

Peg dolls

Peg dolls were the little sisters of Dutch or, more correctly, Deutsch dolls that came from Germany. They were much loved by Victorian children who knew them as penny woodens and wooden Bettys. Suitably dressed for their differing domestic roles, they were often to be found at home, below stairs, in the large dolls' houses of the period.

Dolly pegs can still be bought very cheaply today.

30

To make one you need:
a dolly peg (from Woolworths)
paints or felt tipped pens
a scrap of fabric or a paper dishcloth
fabric adhesive such as Copydex
a cocktail stick or two matchsticks
unravelled string or snippets of hair or fur (for hair)
a paper doiley
a pair of small scissors
any small trimmings such as feathers, beads, ribbon,
    confetti, silver or tinted cake decorations

See that the peg is facing front and paint or draw a face on it. As the peg is so small this looks much better if it is kept simple – perhaps two dots for the eyes, a small red 'v' for the mouth and two pretty pink cheeks.

Put some adhesive round the peg, fairly high up, for the waistline. Then cut a rather long rectangle of fabric and, starting at the back of the peg, bunch it round evenly to make a skirt. Hold it in place on the glue for a moment. Then put a little adhesive down the edge of the back seam and stick the back together. Trim the skirt to the length you want.

Cut a curved piece of doiley to make a bodice and stick it round tightly to hold the skirt firmly in place.

Take the two matchsticks or, if you are using a cocktail stick, cut it in half, to make the arms. Cut two strips of material and paste them round the sticks leaving a small part visible at one end for the hand. Trim off the overlap.

Put two large dots of adhesive on the shoulders and leave them to set for a few minutes.

Now press the arms firmly onto the dots of adhesive with the sleeve seams to the inside where they won't show.

Cut another curve from the doiley, slightly larger than the one you cut for the bodice, to make a shawl. Stick it round, slightly crossing over in front. This ensures that the arms are held firmly.

Make a paper doiley bow for the back of the dress and stick it in place.

34

Colour in the hat-tie on the face and chest and also colour in the shoes.

Put adhesive round the sides and back of the head and stick on the hair. Leave it to set for a few moments, then trim it to the length you want. Trim the hair neatly round the top edge too.

Cut a piece of doiley for the crown of the hat and another for a brim as shown in the picture. Then pleat the brim onto the crown, sticking it round to fit.

Cut two long thin strips of fabric, tie one in a bow and stick the the other round for a hatband. Trim the ends and stick the bow onto the front of the hat.

Trimmings can now be added where you wish. You could make many more peg dolls using your own ideas for different ways of dressing them.

35

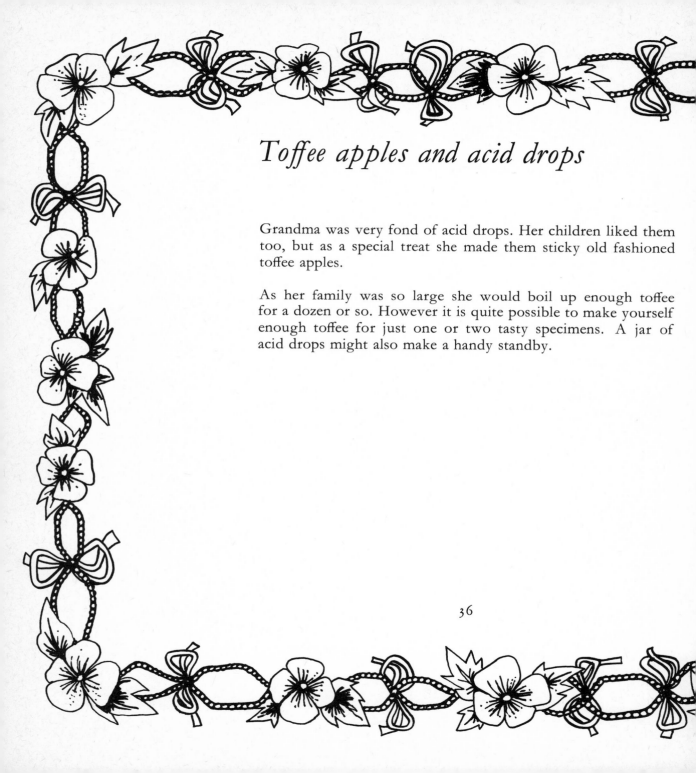

Toffee apples and acid drops

Grandma was very fond of acid drops. Her children liked them too, but as a special treat she made them sticky old fashioned toffee apples.

As her family was so large she would boil up enough toffee for a dozen or so. However it is quite possible to make yourself enough toffee for just one or two tasty specimens. A jar of acid drops might also make a handy standby.

To make four toffee apples you need:
a large cup of Demerara sugar
two tablespoons of butter
a tablespoon of water
one tablespoon of vinegar
four firm apples
four clean sticks (skewers or steel knitting needles
    will do if you haven't any wooden sticks)
a sheet of buttered paper
a strong saucepan with a thick bottom
a wooden spoon and a basin of cold water
an old leather or rubber glove might be useful
    for the hand that holds the stick

Wash the apples but do not peel them. Poke the sticks firmly into them. Do not be tempted to waggle them about at this stage or you will loose your apple in the hot toffee.

Put the sugar, butter and water into the pan and heat it very gently to dissolve the sugar. Heat it as slowly as you can. Do not try to hurry.

When the sugar is dissolved, add the vinegar and increase the heat, and stirring with the wooden spoon, bring the mixture to the boil.

Do not stir in a splashy sort of way. Just keep the spoon moving over the bottom of the pan to make sure the toffee does not stick to it and start to burn.

Gradually it will change from a golden colour to a rich brown. Do not let it become a very dark brown, or your apples will have a bitter taste.

When you have a delicious-looking toffee apple colour, turn off the heat and put your basin of water near the pan.

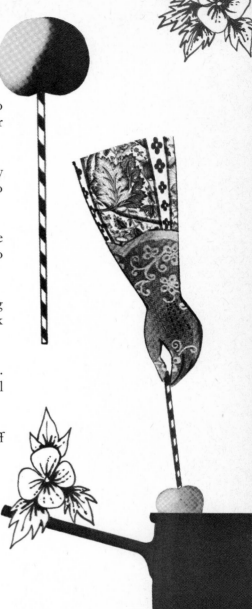

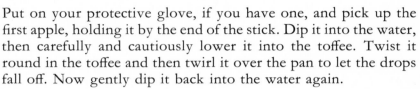

Put on your protective glove, if you have one, and pick up the first apple, holding it by the end of the stick. Dip it into the water, then carefully and cautiously lower it into the toffee. Twist it round in the toffee and then twirl it over the pan to let the drops fall off. Now gently dip it back into the water again.

Do all this again to give it a second coat – water, toffee, water. Then give it a little shake and lay it down on the buttered paper.

Make the rest in the same way. If the toffee starts to stiffen in the pan, gently heat it up again. As it gets used up, tip the pan slightly as you twist and twirl the apple.

The toffee apples are best eaten fairly soon as the good old-fashioned kind go sticky if they are kept too long.

Acid drops

To make these you need: two cups of sugar, half a cup of water, a quarter of a teaspoon of cream of tartar, three drops of lemon essence, two teaspoons of tartaric acid (from the chemist), a pair of scissors, a strong pan, a broad knife, a wooden spoon and a large oiled slab.

Put the sugar, water and cream of tartar in the pan and boil the mixture gently until it becomes a pale yellow colour.

Remove it from the heat and stir in the lemon essence.

Taking very great care, pour it slowly onto the middle of the oiled slab. Try to keep it in the centre with your knife. (If it still threatens to run over the side, put some back in the saucepan and make a little at a time.)

Sprinkle the tartaric acid over it and work it in with the knife.

As soon as it is cool enough to handle, roll it into thin rolls. Working as quickly as you can, cut up the rolls into small pieces and roll them into balls under your hand. Sprinkle them with sifted sugar, let them dry well, and store them in a jar.

41

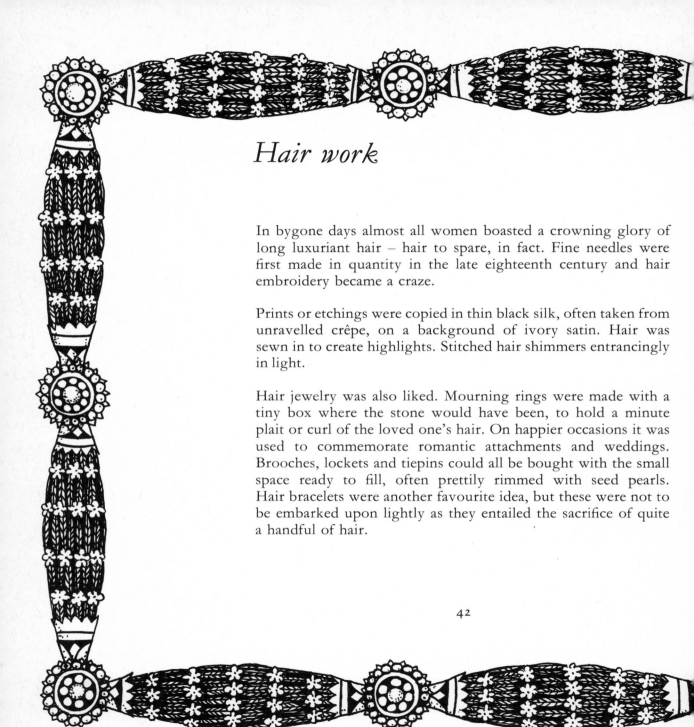

Hair work

In bygone days almost all women boasted a crowning glory of long luxuriant hair – hair to spare, in fact. Fine needles were first made in quantity in the late eighteenth century and hair embroidery became a craze.

Prints or etchings were copied in thin black silk, often taken from unravelled crêpe, on a background of ivory satin. Hair was sewn in to create highlights. Stitched hair shimmers entrancingly in light.

Hair jewelry was also liked. Mourning rings were made with a tiny box where the stone would have been, to hold a minute plait or curl of the loved one's hair. On happier occasions it was used to commemorate romantic attachments and weddings. Brooches, lockets and tiepins could all be bought with the small space ready to fill, often prettily rimmed with seed pearls. Hair bracelets were another favourite idea, but these were not to be embarked upon lightly as they entailed the sacrifice of quite a handful of hair.

42

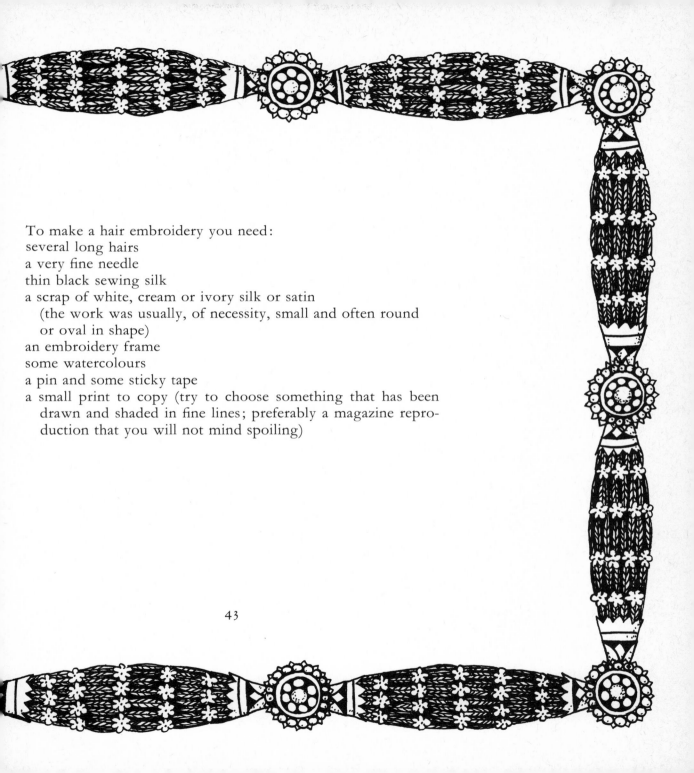

To make a hair embroidery you need:
several long hairs
a very fine needle
thin black sewing silk
a scrap of white, cream or ivory silk or satin
    (the work was usually, of necessity, small and often round
    or oval in shape)
an embroidery frame
some watercolours
a pin and some sticky tape
a small print to copy (try to choose something that has been
    drawn and shaded in fine lines; preferably a magazine repro-
    duction that you will not mind spoiling)

RUBENS.

Stretch your material in the frame and see that it is held firmly in place.

Lay the print on top of it, holding it steady with a little sticky tape.

Take the pin and carefully prick through all the main lines of the print so that it transfers the picture to the material in a series of easily seen pinpricks.

Remove the print and keep it by your side to copy.

Use the black silk for embroidering most of the picture, and keep the hairs to use as highlights. Try using three or four hairs at once. Surprisingly, even black hair will look quite light against the black silk.

Now you can embroider your picture using long and short straight stitches where appropriate and also little dots for speckling effects. There are no set stitches, so you can be quite inventive. It was usual in Victorian times for the lady to practise new ideas on the spare edges left out of the frame. Often, when these works are removed from their frames these little experiments come to light.

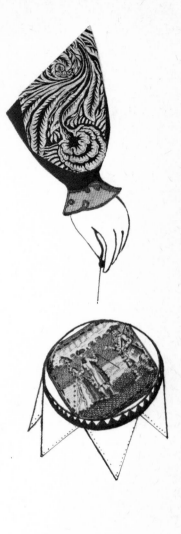

45

Use the silk and hair as you like. Very pale water colour washes can also be added to the picture to tint faces or the sky. Again it is advisable to try this out first on a corner or spare scrap of material.

When you have finished, remove the embroidery from the frame and press it with a cool iron under a damp cloth.

If you would like to make your picture oval or round but have no suitable frame, you might like to imitate the 'Verre Eglomise' frame, often used for these embroideries.

To make one you need: a square or rectangular frame, thick black paint, and some gold paint or liquid-leaf.

Paint two or three coats of black on the wrong side of the glass, leaving an oval or round space in the middle, the right size for the picture.

When it is quite dry, scratch a decorative flower or similar pretty design in each of the four corners.

Blow away any dust and then carefully paint it in, again on the wrong side, with gold.

.46

If you have a steady hand you could also paint a fine gold rim round the centre space. If you have an unsteady one, paint it in and scratch off the bits you don't want when it is dry. Turn it over and it is ready for your picture.

If you do not have a great deal of time and patience to spare, you could try a smaller embroidery. Young ladies used to embroider the initials of their lovers in their own hair on the corners of cambric and fine lawn handkerchiefs.

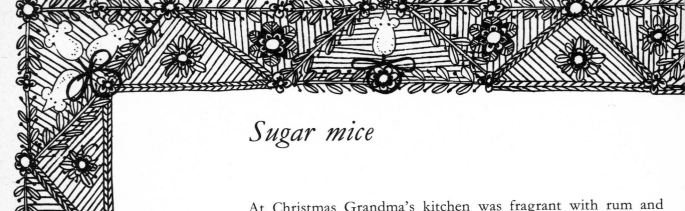

Sugar mice

At Christmas Grandma's kitchen was fragrant with rum and spices and a fairyland of iced biscuits and sweets. Sugar mice were always a favourite. The Christmas tree was first brought from Germany by Prince Albert, and this fashion set by the royal family was quickly copied by all. The trees were decorated mostly with home-made fare and these delightful little creatures, with extra long tails, dangled from the branches – Not for long though; they tasted too good!

48

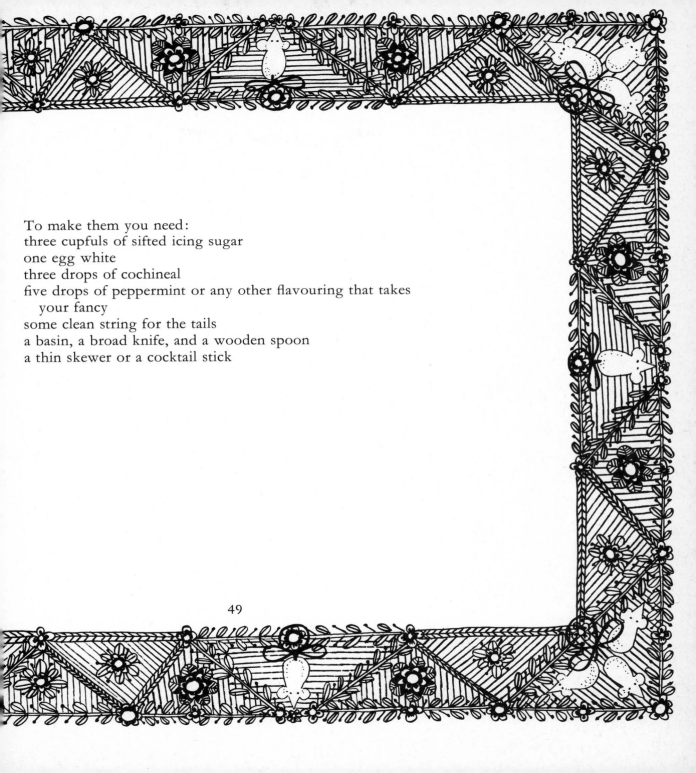

To make them you need:
three cupfuls of sifted icing sugar
one egg white
three drops of cochineal
five drops of peppermint or any other flavouring that takes
   your fancy
some clean string for the tails
a basin, a broad knife, and a wooden spoon
a thin skewer or a cocktail stick

49

Put the egg white into a basin and add to it your three drops of cochineal and five drops of flavouring. Beat these lightly together with the wooden spoon until the colour looks fairly even.

Start adding the icing sugar a little at a time, beating it in until you have a smooth, stiff pink mixture.

Sprinkle some icing sugar onto your hands and start kneading it into a large firm ball.

If it still seems too sticky to work, add a little more sifted icing sugar.

Find a clean dry surface to work on, and divide the mixture into small mouse-shaped lumps. Do not make them too big as they are quite rich to eat. Make them round at the back end and pointed at the front. Also leave a small amount of the mixture on one side for making the ears.

To make the ears, roll the mixture into small balls and then press your finger onto each in turn, pinching them together slightly at the bottom.

It is a good plan to work fairly quickly at this stage as your mice will become hard and firm quite quickly.

51

Stick the ears firmly in place. Prick small holes with a skewer for the eyes and tail.

Cut up your string into lengths for the tails. Dip the end of the tail in water and put it in the tail hole, pinching the hole together for a tight fit.

Ease the mice off the working surface very gently with the broad knife and leave them on a plate to set for a few hours.

Fondant mice

Sugar mice can also be made of fondant. They look more like the professional mice you see sometimes in shops, but are slightly more difficult to make.

To make them by this method you need:
450 grammes (1 lb.) of granulated sugar.
a cupful of water.
three drops of cochineal and five of flavouring
$1\frac{1}{2}$ teaspoons of glucose or a good pinch of cream of tartar
a good strong pan
a large wetted or oiled slab
a broad knife

Great care must always be taken when making sweets from boiled sugar.

Put the sugar and water into the pan and heat it very gently until the sugar dissolves. This stage cannot be hurried.

When it has dissolved, add your colouring, flavouring and also the glucose or cream of tartar. Bring it to the boil and continue boiling it until it reaches a temperature of 237°F. This is known as 'small ball'. If you spoon out a few drops, let them cool for a moment, put your fingers under the cold tap and then find you can roll your sample into a small ball, you can be sure the correct stage has been reached.

It is always a good plan to take the pan off the heat whilst making this sort of test so that it does not get too hot.

When 'small ball' has been reached, pour the mixture very carefully indeed into the middle of your large oiled or wetted slab, keeping it in the middle with the broad knife. If it threatens to run over the edge, leave some of the mixture in the pan and use just a small quantity at a time.

Let the mixture cool slightly, then work it well with the knife. As it cools more, knead it with your hands. Then make up your sugar mice as you did with the icing sugar.

53

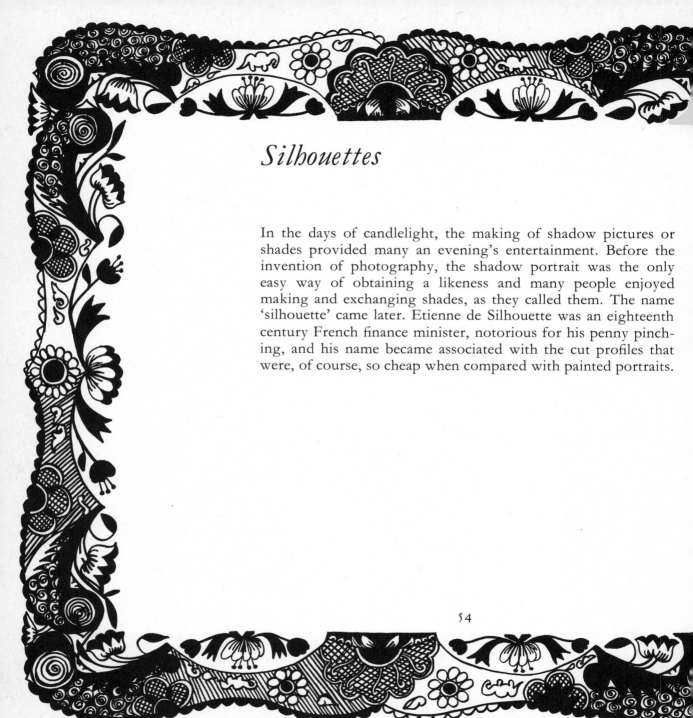

Silhouettes

In the days of candlelight, the making of shadow pictures or shades provided many an evening's entertainment. Before the invention of photography, the shadow portrait was the only easy way of obtaining a likeness and many people enjoyed making and exchanging shades, as they called them. The name 'silhouette' came later. Etienne de Silhouette was an eighteenth century French finance minister, notorious for his penny pinching, and his name became associated with the cut profiles that were, of course, so cheap when compared with painted portraits.

To make a silhouette you need:
a large sheet of white paper (for economy, a roll of lining wall-
    paper is very good value)
a sheet of black paper
a table lamp with a long flex
a pair of small pointed scissors
a sharp pencil, some sticky tape, two drawing-pins
a friend who can sit still without fidgeting

Pin your white paper on the wall and place your friend, in a high backed chair if possible, a few feet away from it . The lamp should be behind him.

If you don't have a suitable chair to steady his head, you might try putting a table in front of him and letting him rest his elbow on it, supporting his chin with a finger.

Take a little time moving your sitter and the lamp until you have a crisp shadow of his profile thrown onto the paper.

Take your sharp pencil and draw carefully and accurately round the shadow. Your friend must keep very still indeed.

Now remove the paper. Stick the black paper behind the drawing with sticky tape and carefully cut through both layers together. You now have a black shadow portrait.

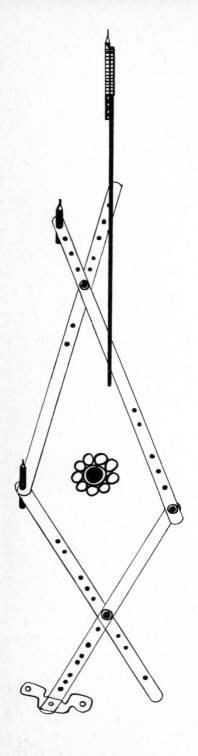

You might like to try another way of producing a profile drawing.

Tape your pencil to a thin but rigid rod about 30 cm. (12 in.) long. Make sure there's no wobble. Sit your victim near the paper on the wall and simply draw round his profile, resting the rod lightly on his face as you go.

You can turn the likenesses into miniatures with a pantograph, which works on a trellis principle. You put two pencils in specially placed slots and whilst you trace round your large profile, the other pencil draws the same outline on a smaller scale. Pantographs can be bought at most good stationers and art shops.

You can finish the portraits in many different ways. You can touch in hair and detail of dress lightly with gold or pale grey. Soldiers in dress uniform were often coloured in completely, except for the face.

A white collar looks crisp if it is cut out completely so that the mounting paper shows through.

Sometimes people used to cut out the whole thing from white paper and then stick the black paper behind the space. These are known as hollow-cut silhouettes.

58

For a rather expensive looking mosaic effect, you can break eggshells into tiny pieces and stick them inside the profile, paying special attention to the edge.

When you become an expert you will be able to try full length portraits and family groups. As practice makes perfect, of course, you will soon discard your pencil and lamp and, using your trained eye, cut them out freehand.

Clapperboard

When the children were ill, they were rubbed until they glowed with camphorated oil and spent the day tucked up in the big brass-knobbed feather bed. Then Grandma would bring out the best thing of all – her box of tricks.

It was a treasure chest of exciting things – squeaking buns that looked unquestionably real, green velvet clockwork frogs, the Lord's prayer written on the back of a tiny silver threepenny bit, the smallest doll in the world, and all kinds of tricks and puzzles.

A teaser among these was the mysterious clapperboard.

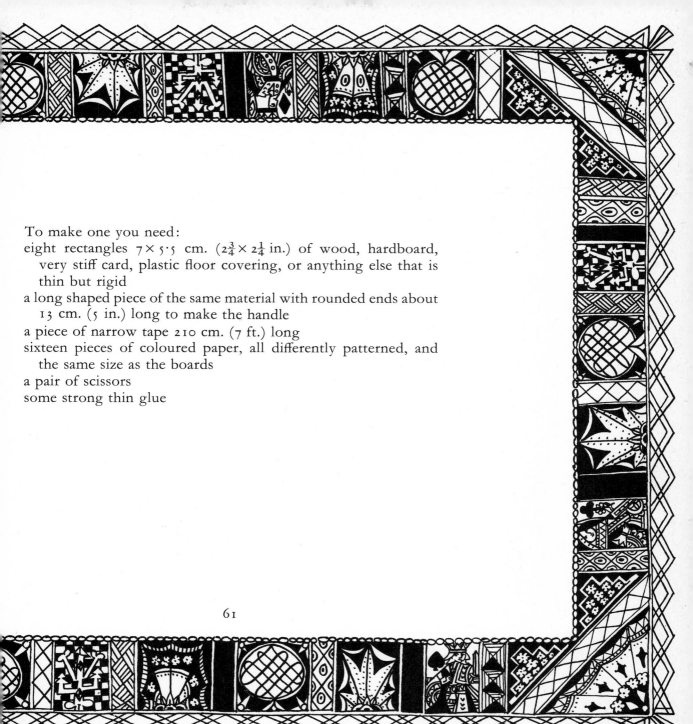

To make one you need:

eight rectangles $7 \times 5\cdot5$ cm. ($2\frac{3}{4} \times 2\frac{1}{4}$ in.) of wood, hardboard, very stiff card, plastic floor covering, or anything else that is thin but rigid

a long shaped piece of the same material with rounded ends about 13 cm. (5 in.) long to make the handle

a piece of narrow tape 210 cm. (7 ft.) long

sixteen pieces of coloured paper, all differently patterned, and the same size as the boards

a pair of scissors

some strong thin glue

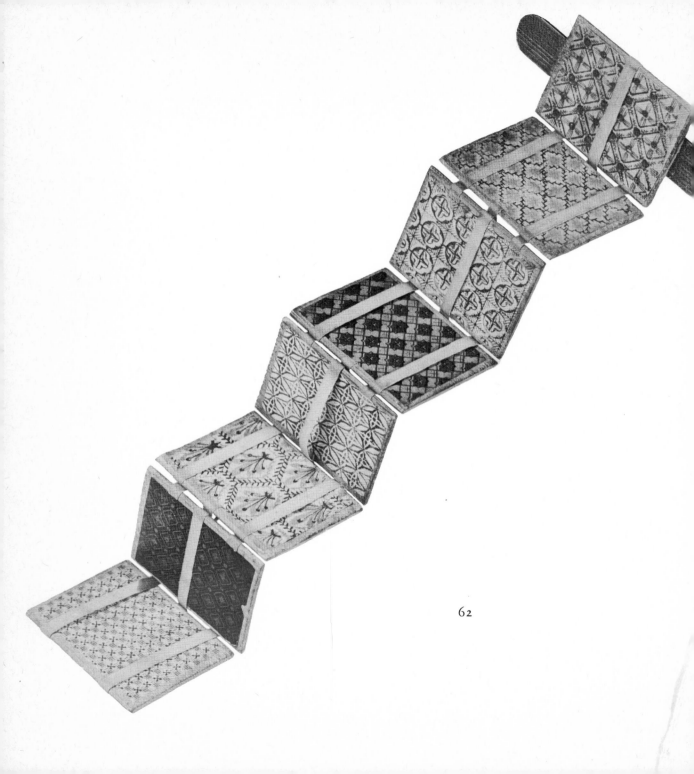

Lay your eight boards side by side in a row, with the longer sides together, almost touching each other.

Glue your handle piece across the middle of the first board and let it overlap equally at each side.

Cut the tape into twenty-one pieces 10 cm. (4 in.) long.

Take the first nine and stick the ends to the boards as shown in the drawing. The dotted lines show where the tapes are stuck behind the boards and the black lines show where they lie free and loose over the front.

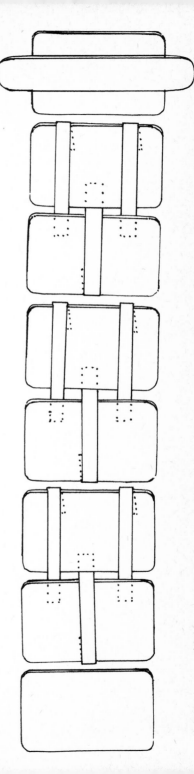

63

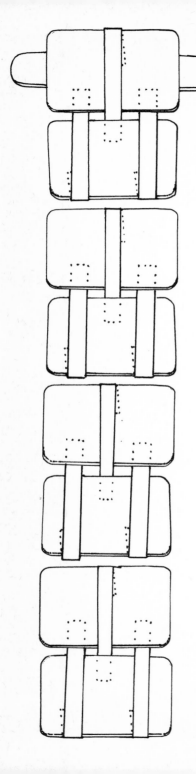

Carefully turn the boards over and stick the ends of the remaining twelve tapes in the positions shown in the second picture, again making sure that you stick the ends behind the boards and let the loose lengths lie over the front.

Stick your coloured papers onto the boards, sliding them under the loose tape but covering the stuck down ends.

Now your clapperboard is ready to use. Hold the handle in both hands with the front towards you. Turn the first board backward against the second one and, as Grandma used to say, you might surprise yourself.